C000261784

30 DAYS TO A STRONGER CHILD

Educate and Empower Kids would like to acknowledge the following people who contributed time, talents and energy to this publication.

Dina Alexander, MS
Jenny Webb, MA
Amanda Scott
Mary Ann Benson, MSW, LSW
Polly Scott, MEd

Ed Allison
Cliff Park, MBA

Design and Illustration By:
Jera Mehrdad

For great resources and information, follow us:

www.educateempowerkids.org
Facebook: www.facebook.com/educateempowerkids/
Twitter: @EduEmpowerKids
Pinterest: pinterest.com/educateempower/
Instagram: Eduempowerkids

Rising Parent Media, LLC

© 2016 by Rising Parent Media

All rights reserved. Published 2016

Printed in the United States of America

20 19 18 17 16   1 2 3 4

ISBN: 978-0-9863708-9-2 (paperback)

ISBN: 978-0-9863708-3-0 (e-book)

The paper used in this publication meets the minimum requirements of the American National Standard for Information Sciences—Permanence of Paper for Printed Library Materials, ANSI Z39.48-1992.

Subscribe to our website for exclusive offers and information at:
www.educateempowerkids.org

TABLE OF CONTENTS

INTRODUCTION

OUR GOAL: to provide tools to facilitate meaningful conversations and experience-based learning opportunities that will help you connect with your kids.

Everyone has various internal qualities that need to be developed and balanced in order to function. When we work to develop each of these qualities, we not only function, we thrive. We learn, we adapt, we grow, we share, and we find our greatness.

Each of these qualities—Physical, Emotional, Social, Spiritual, and Intellectual—is important and necessary to live a healthy, balanced, and strong life.

We can think about developing these qualities in terms of maintaining an account balance. Our children face pressures that can deplete these accounts. It is our job to teach our kids to be aware of what will deplete these accounts and what we can do to keep them at sufficient levels. If our kids don't learn to keep their accounts full, they won't have the inner strength to resist outside pressures.

Pressures faced by our kids: to conform, to avoid challenges, to lose hope, to give up, to push down feelings, to not follow one's heart or mind, to not stand up for self and for others, to be lazy.

When one account is empty, we borrow from other accounts. For example, when a person feels lonely or upset, he may overeat to try to fill his account—borrowing from his physical account to fill his emotional account. When several accounts are low, we experience anxiety, sadness, and even depression.

A STRONG CHILD IS RESILIENT AND CAN RESIST OUTSIDE PRESSURES. SHE IS ABLE TO WITHSTAND OR RECOVER QUICKLY FROM CHANGE OR DIFFICULT CONDITIONS.

As you enjoy these lessons with your children, you will connect with them on a new level. Connecting is the process of developing care and concern for another person. This connection facilitates learning and bonding, and together you will help your child construct a life script.

One of the most important jobs we have as parents is to help our children develop a script to live by. Sometimes this development is accomplished as we teach necessary life skills, such as how to drive a car or how to tie shoes. Sometimes this is done by accumulated example, such as the way you speak when upset. Your tone, the way you handle stress, or how you handle an argument with your neighbor all work together to build a model for your child to imitate.

This life script helps them know what to do when they have a choice or need to make a decision—both mundane, daily decisions and vital choices for their future. We cannot give our children a complete instruction book with an answer for every situation. We can give them a foundation consisting of strong guidelines and principled code that will help them think for themselves as they assess their life choices so that they can both function and thrive in society.

USING THIS BOOK

This book is designed to facilitate thirty conversations regarding five important qualities in order to help your child fill and balance their accounts. You can work through the sections sequentially or skip around—whatever best fits your child's needs.

Each of the five sections—Physical, Emotional, Social, Spiritual, and Intellectual—is divided into six lessons. The lessons are designed as a self-contained conversation for you and your child. Each lesson is organized into the following sections:

EDUCATE: We provide a brief orientation to the topic, including why it's important for your child's development and how to make them stronger.

COMMUNICATE: This section includes potential conversation topics instigated by questions and activities designed to connect you and your child as you discuss the topic.

NURTURE: This section includes additional activities and dialogues for deeper engagement between parent and child.

EMPOWER: This section contains additional challenges designed to apply the skills and understanding learned through the discussion and activities.

These conversations are designed to adapt to your needs. If you only have five minutes, that will work! Hit the highlights, ask a question or two, and know that you can always return to the material later. If you want to really dig into a topic, there is plenty of material here to engage you both and help you connect.

We encourage you to try a dialogue or do an activity. There are activities of all types—some for learning, some that are to be done together, and others that challenge your child to accomplish something. Each of these is meant to bring you and your child closer together as you experience life together, grow together, and create a stronger life script.

You can do this! We know our children are strong—let's help them realize and develop that strength in a fun and encouraging environment. We're with you all the way!

For additional ideas and information, come visit us at educateempowerkids.org.

SOCIAL ACCOUNT

INTRODUCTION

Developing strong social skills is key to a child's personal development. Of course, some children have a tendency to be shy while others are more outgoing—one isn't necessarily better than the other—but children can learn to use their strengths.

Some children seem to be social creatures from the time they are born while others may struggle with making friends. There is no question that children who have good social skills will have advantages in life. Children who possess good social tools not only have the benefit of positive relationships, they have a better self-image and, in general, are much more resilient as they face life's challenges.

Luckily, friend-making, assertiveness, and confidence are things that can be taught. Environment can play a huge role in helping a child practice using her social tools because social skills are, of course, best learned in a social environment.

In this section, children will gain tools to use in social settings and discover within themselves their social strengths, what makes them great friends, and how to choose friends wisely.

ACCOUNTABILITY
"ACCOUNTABILITY BREEDS
RESPONSE-ABILITY."
– STEPHEN COVEY

📖 **EDUCATE:** Accountability is an important skill because it shows that a person accepts that they are responsible for their own actions. They acknowledge that they have some control over their life's choices and the way their actions affect others. When we practice personal accountability, we begin to think through our actions ahead of time and start to use more self-control. Every child is accountable for using the opportunities they are given wisely.

❓ **COMMUNICATE:** Use the following questions to help your child understand that as they mature and grow, they'll be able to find resolutions to problems without consulting others, like parents. Be sure to let your child know that even though you are encouraging their independence, you will always be available to them.

DISCUSSION QUESTIONS

Can you think of a time when you took responsibility for something negative that you did? (This is holding yourself accountable.)

Why is it necessary to be honest with yourself when it comes to accountability?

What are ways that you can show that you accept responsibility for your actions?

What if your actions lead to unintended consequences? Are you still responsible for those consequences?

♥ NURTURE: It's important to be accountable for our actions so that we can continue to be trustworthy people. Sometimes it is easier to blame others for our mistakes or make excuses for our actions than to take responsibility for them. As we are given opportunities in life (for example, an education or a special privilege), it is wise to consider how to make the most of the opportunity, to be grateful for it, and to show that gratitude.

Activity: Have your child think of a time when they told the truth about something even when they could have gotten away with a lie. How did it make them feel to take responsibility for their actions?

Activity: Ask your child to share something they are responsible for. Ask them what would happen if they didn't fulfill this responsibility. For example: They're responsible for taking out the trash. If they don't, the trash will pile up and become smelly and messy. Or maybe they're responsible for feeding the family pet. If they don't do it, the pet will be hungry.

👑 EMPOWER: Challenge your child to be accountable for a specific action for one week. Help them recognize their accountability by providing a way for them to record each instance in which they fulfill that specific responsibility (like a checklist, chore chart, etc.). The responsibility can be large or small, depending on your child's individual abilities. For example, you may challenge them to brush their teeth each night or to collect the mail every day, or something involving more responsibility, such as picking up a younger sibling from school or planning and preparing a family dinner.

FRIENDSHIP
"FRIENDS ARE THE FAMILY YOU CHOOSE"
- JESS C. SCOTT

📖 **EDUCATE:** Making friends is a skill that comes naturally to some, but not to all. Thankfully, it is a skill that can be learned. Friendship: a relationship of mutual affection between two or more people. The goal of friendship is not to have many friends, but instead to have a few good friends. Every person will have many friendships throughout life. Some will last and others won't. There are qualities that help make some friendships last longer than others, like common interests or shared experiences. There are things that can ruin friendships, like jealousy or hurt feelings.

Q **COMMUNICATE:** Having true friends who you can count on is more important than whether you are popular or not. Encourage your child not to limit him- or herself to one group of friends.

DISCUSSION QUESTIONS
What makes someone a good friend?

What kind of friend do you want to be?

How do you know when a relationship has real value?

What can we do to build healthy relationships?

Do you need a lot of friends to be happy?

What do you think about cliques?

Think about the best friends you've had. Have they supported you? Have they accepted you just as you are?

Often children make friends due to circumstances out of their control (for example, they are in the same school class or their parents are friends). While this isn't bad, it does not help a child understand that they do have a choice when it comes to friendships. Start now by helping them to think about friendship as something they have some control over.

DISCUSSION QUESTIONS

Who is your best friend and what do you like about him?

Do you treat your friends the way your best friend treats you?

How could you be a better friend?

❤ **NURTURE:** We don't have to be friends with everyone, but we do have to respect everyone. We don't have to be friends with people who are unkind to us. We deserve to be treated well. Consider how friendships change and grow. It's important to be patient with someone as your friendship grows.

Activity: Have your child pretend to meet you for the first time. How will they decide if they'd like to be friends? How will they show that they are a good friend? Ask your child how they could determine whether or not they should be friends with someone (what do they have in common, what do they enjoy doing together?).

Activity: Help your child role-play things in a friendship that are unacceptable to them or "dealbreakers" (for example, lying, stealing, gossiping, etc.). Help your child understand that sometimes friendships don't work out. Ask your child, "How would you decide if you should or should not be friends with someone anymore?"

◢◣ **EMPOWER:** Challenge your child to make one new friend in the upcoming week. Remind them to choose this friend wisely and think through their decision beforehand. Maybe they will decide who their new friend will be based on a need they see (such as a lonely person), an instinct they have (a feeling that someone needs a friend), or simply someone they think they might like to know better.

RESPECT

"WE SHOULD ALL CONSIDER EACH
OTHER AS HUMAN BEINGS, AND WE
SHOULD RESPECT EACH OTHER."
— MALALA YOUSAFZAI

📖 **EDUCATE: Respect:** *a feeling or understanding that some-one or something is important and should be treated in an appro-priate way.* Showing respect for others means we listen to other people and treat them the way we want to be treated, even when we disagree. Everyone deserves to be treated with respect and everyone wants to be liked. Finding a way to get along with all types of people is a skill that can greatly benefit your life.

💬 **COMMUNICATE:** Help your child understand the importance of compromise. It's necessary to compromise when people can't agree on something. Learning to compromise is a skill that will help your child get along better with others and strengthen their emotional bonds.

DISCUSSION QUESTIONS

Should you put someone down because he or she has a different opinion, religion, or culture than you do?

Do you know someone who believes something different than you do? Or who has a different idea about how things work?

Can you think of a time you had a problem with someone and you worked it out so that you both felt good?

Let's talk about the different kinds of people we know. What makes us different? What makes us the same?

❤ **NURTURE:** It's very common for children (especially younger children) to see the world in fairly black and white terms. This can make things like compromise and respect for differences a difficult concept to understand. Help your child realize that it's okay to not agree on everything. Teach them that they don't always have to be friends with others, but they do have to treat them with respect.

Activity: Ask your child for an example of a respectful act (listening, following rules). Have them tell you about someone who believes differently than they do, then role-play expressing their opinion and beliefs without bullying or getting angry when someone doesn't agree with them.

Activity: Ask your child to pretend there is something you disagree on. (Don't be surprised if they pick something you actually don't agree about!) Next, ask them to think of a respectful way you both can "agree to disagree" and still remain friends.

◣ **EMPOWER:** Parents should acknowledge that there are differences between their child and their child's friends. Point out things the children enjoy doing together despite those differences. Challenge your child to find things in common with people they aren't close to. For instance, maybe there is a person with whom your child has never had a close relationship, but they both enjoy drawing, love animals, or eating peanut butter and jelly at lunch. For every difference people can find, there is likely a commonality as well. Parents can acknowledge the differences among family members. Even in families, people don't agree on everything.

ASSERTIVENESS

"THE BASIC DIFFERENCE BETWEEN BEING ASSERTIVE AND BEING AGGRESSIVE IS HOW OUR WORDS AND BEHAVIOR AFFECT THE RIGHTS AND WELL BEING OF OTHERS."
    – SHARON ANTHONY BOWER

📖 **EDUCATE:** **Assertiveness:** *characterized by bold or confident statements and behavior.* Being assertive in a positive way is a skill that will benefit every child throughout their lifetime. At every age, there are times when a child will need to stand up for themselves and for others. The ability to handle these instances can shape the course of a young child's life. Every child must learn that they have certain rights that should never be violated. Standing up for other's rights is another way for a child to assert themselves positively. It's important to understand the difference between assertiveness and aggressiveness.

🗩 **COMMUNICATE:** Assertive people state their opinions while still being respectful of others and without making those around them feel powerless or unimportant. Aggressive people attack or ignore others' opinions in favor of their own, feel their thoughts are the most important, and need to feel powerful. Passive people don't state their opinions at all. Use the following questions to discuss these differences with your child.

DISCUSSION QUESTIONS

What is the difference between feeling powerful (assertive) and powerless?

What can we do to feel powerful and confident while not making others feel powerless?

What can we do if we feel powerless or intimidated?

Can you identify times you've needed to stand up for yourself? What was easy about it? What was hard?

What does it mean to follow the Golden Rule? (The Golden Rule means we always treat people the way we'd like to be treated.)

What qualifies as bullying?

If you think you have bullied others in the past, how do you think you could change your behavior?

♥ **NURTURE:** We have a duty as respectful people to stand up for others. In childhood, opportunities to stand up for themselves and for others often occur in bullying situations. Explain to your child that bullying can be physical and/or verbal. Assertiveness can be useful when dealing with a bullying situation, but children should know when to make an adult aware of the situation.

Activity: Discuss the following scenario with your child. "You are walking home from school and you find two older kids making fun of your friend. How would you stand up for your friend?" Talk about how to know when a bullying situation requires an adult's help (for example, if the bully has become violent or hateful).

Activity: Invite your child to play a game with you. Any type of game will do (board game, card game, video game, or even a sports challenge like Horse or scoring goals). Enjoy your time together, but also don't hold back too much during the game. If they start to lose their temper or get upset, help them to find positive ways to change that negative assertiveness into positive assertiveness. For example, instead of whining, they could issue a teasing challenge like "Well, next time I'm going to win!"

👑 **EMPOWER:** Challenge your child to be assertive. Stress the difference between assertiveness and aggressiveness. If they have an opportunity to be assertive and stand up for themselves or others in a positive way, have them tell you about it and compliment them on their strength to use positive assertiveness.

LEADERSHIP

"IF YOUR ACTIONS INSPIRE OTHERS TO DREAM MORE, LEARN MORE, DO MORE AND BECOME MORE, YOU ARE A LEADER."
– JOHN QUINCY ADAMS

📖 **EDUCATE:** **Leadership:** *the power or ability to lead other people.* Anyone can be a leader. Sometimes children assume that a person needs to be loud or mean to be a leader, but this is, of course, false. A person with good ideas who is able to guide others and motivate them to work with positive reinforcement is a good leader. Leaders are able to communicate their needs and are willing to listen to others' needs as well. Some children may have the natural inclination to lead, but any child can learn to lead!

Q **COMMUNICATE:** Every child needs role models. Teach your child to choose their heroes and role models wisely. Teach them to look for qualities they would like to grow and develop within themselves. Qualities that strengthen leadership include authenticity, creativity, perseverance, teamwork, and humility.

DISCUSSION QUESTIONS

What do you think a good leader does?
Do you know any good leaders?

What type of person would you want to follow?
What qualities do you have that make you a good leader?

What leadership qualities would you like to develop?

Are there bad leaders? How do they behave?

♥ **NURTURE:** We need to teach our children not to be afraid to speak up when they have a "light bulb moment"—some of the best ideas have come from brainstorming! At the same time, it's important to listen to the suggestions of others that might improve upon the original idea. Remind your child that we don't have to be the leader every time.

SAMPLE DIALOGUE

Parent: "Let's practice saying things a leader might say in a respectful way."

Child: "I don't know. 'Good job.' Stuff like that."

Parent: "How about things like 'Why don't we try it this way?' and 'This might work better if …'"

Child: "But then I can't make them do it my way!"

Parent: "Being a good leader isn't about making people do things, it's about encouraging them and helping them see things in a new way."

Activity: Have your child pick a skill they're really good at and then ask them to teach you how to do it (for example, making paper airplanes, throwing a baseball, drawing animals, building spaceships, etc.). Point out to them that as they are teaching you they are developing their leadership skills. They have to communicate their information and keep you interested in the activity—that's being a leader!

Activity: Ask your child to select a person they consider to be a role model in their life. Ask them why they chose that person and talk about what makes them a good role model and leader. Does she have the qualities of a good leader previously listed?

▬ **EMPOWER:** Challenge your child to choose and read a biography of someone they admire as a leader—even a picture book biography. Discuss the biography with them afterwards, asking them particularly what they felt the biography taught them about leadership and what they admired about the person.

BOUNDARIES
"BOUNDARIES ASSIST ME TO
REMAIN HEALTHY, HONEST AND LIVING
A LIFE THAT IS TRUE TO ME."
– LEE HORBACHEWSKI

📖 **EDUCATE:** We all have boundaries, both physical and emotional. **Boundaries:** *the unofficial rules about what should not be done and limits that define acceptable behavior in a relationship.* For example, someone we know quite well may stand closer to us than a stranger. We share personal information and feelings with people we know well that we don't share with strangers. Not all people are trustworthy, and it's important for children to understand that there are different levels of trust among the people we know. They might feel comfortable hugging one person but not another. Help them understand that they have the right to decide who is allowed in their personal space and private thoughts.

💬 **COMMUNICATE:** Discuss the personal space within your family and how it differs from interactions with those outside of your immediate family. Make sure your child knows that they may set their own standards for personal space and information. Talk about how relationships can evolve over time, starting with the widest circle and progressing inward with time and increased trust.

DISCUSSION QUESTIONS

What is something you might tell a friend that you wouldn't tell someone you just met?

How do you greet someone when meeting her for the first time?

How do we classify people we only know online into the personal space areas? (These people should all be placed in our "public circle.")

How do you know when a person is a close friend, acquaintance, or a stranger?

How might people that you are close to violate your personal boundaries, both physically and emotionally?

💜 **NURTURE:** Learning how to firmly yet politely enforce one's boundaries is a skill that takes practice. Help your child develop their confidence through the following activities. Be sure to remind them that they are strong—they can learn to stand up for their boundaries, and by doing so, show others that they respect themselves and others!

Activity: Have your child draw a picture of themselves and draw four circles around it. Explain that the closest circle represents family and extremely close friends, the second circle represents people they are friends with and probably see on a regular basis, the third circle represents acquaintances, and the fourth circle represents strangers. Help them write in the names of people who fit in each category. As you fill out the picture, ask your child how they interact with people in each category. How close should they physically be to their body? What are some things they might confide, or not confide, to each of these people?

Activity: Say to your child, "Let's pretend we have just met. How will you introduce yourself to me? How close will we stand?" Have them practice shaking hands and standing a respectful distance away. With older children, focus on different situations in which they may need to introduce themselves: meeting a new peer, going to a job interview, or meeting the parents of their boyfriend or girlfriend.

Activity: Say to your child, "Pretend I am a person in any of your circles but I am standing too close for your comfort. How will you ask me to move away?" Have them try saying, "You are inside my personal space. Please step back."

🔻 **EMPOWER:** Challenge your child to pay close attention to their boundaries through the course of one day. At the end of the day, help them list out the people they interacted with and then help them put those people into their corresponding circles. Compliment your child on the times they used appropriate social behavior in conjunction with properly assessing their own boundaries.

RESOURCES

MEDIA

Davies, L. (2007). Assertiveness training for children. Retrieved from http://www.kellybear.com/TeacherArticles/TeacherTip74.html.

Riley, J. (2014). 20 personal space activities for kids. Retrieved from http://amomwithalessonplan.com/personal-space-activities-for-kids/.

Dewar, G. (n.d.). Social skills activities for children and teenagers. Retrieved from http://www.parentingscience.com/social-skills-activities.html.

Hurt, K. (2013). 8 ways to nurture leadership in young children. Retrieved from http://letsgrowleaders.com/leadership-in-children/nurture-leadership-in-young-children/.

Pellegrini, A. (2005). The nature of play: Great apes and humans. New York, NY: Guilford Press.

Moss, W. (2011). Being me: A kid's guide to boosting confidence and self-esteem. Washington, DC: Magination Press.

Social Skills Central. (n.d.) All the tools you need to teach lifelong social skills. Retrieved from http://www.socialskillscentral.com/.

ORGANIZATIONS

Character.org
{www.character.org}
Character.org is a nonprofit organization that encourages character development and education in young people.

National Association of School Psychologists
{www.nasponline.org}
The NASP seeks to help school psychologists by giving them resources.

PBS Parents
{www.pbs.org/parents/}
PBS Parents provides resources for understanding social and emotional growth through their Child Development pages.

INTELLECTUAL
ACCOUNT

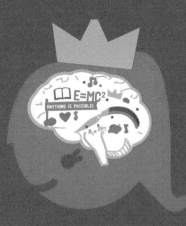

INTRODUCTION

Critical thinking, creative problem solving, and maintaining curiosity are skills that enable our children to successfully face the challenges they will encounter throughout their lives. We want our children to strengthen their intellectual muscles so they can have a happy, productive life. This type of intelligence has little to do with grades or test scores, although good grades and test scores can be important pieces to the overall puzzle. Fostering intelligence means knowing how to apply what's been learned in order to improve a situation or help another person.

The skills associated with intellectual strength are integrated with the other sections discussed so far. All are enhanced through curiosity, creativity, and critical thinking. And, in turn, they contribute to one's overall abilities to foster intellectual strength.

We all have experienced at some point a lack of emotional control or understanding that has clouded our ability to see what is going on and appropriately assess a situation. We have all experienced the mental slowness and confusion that can result after failing to care for our physical needs, such as sleep.

It's important that we teach our children how to care for and value their inherent intelligence while realizing that valuing intellectual health is not the same thing as valuing high test scores or straight As. Every child learns differently and applies knowledge through distinct means. The goal of this section is to help empower you as a parent to teach your child to value their own intelligence and to make choices that will help them to develop habits and patterns that will allow them to reach their full intellectual potential.

By learning to enjoy the rewards of their own intellectual development at an early age, children gain valuable insight and understanding into the ways that learning can enhance one's life long after they have left their formal schooling behind.

CREATIVITY
"THE TRUE SIGN OF INTELLIGENCE IS NOT KNOWLEDGE BUT IMAGINATION." – ALBERT EINSTEIN

📖 **EDUCATE:** **Creativity:** *the ability to transcend traditional ideas and make new things or think of new ideas.* A creative mind is a strong mind. A creative mind is able to look at a problem and see a solution that no one else has thought of yet. A creative mind is willing to take risks and is even willing to fail, knowing that risk and failure alike teach their own lessons. A creative mind is, ultimately, a gift that will allow your child to enjoy the ups and downs in their lives, solve problems, find joy, and connect with other people.

We should foster creativity in our homes and in our families in a variety of ways. We can encourage our children to find their own modes of expression. We can listen to their opinions and respond respectfully, teaching them that their thoughts have worth. We can provide a safe environment for them to make mistakes and fail in so that they have the opportunity to realize that mistakes are another way of learning. We can provide them with enriching activities and materials. And most importantly, we can let them play.

💬 **COMMUNICATE:** Sometimes children can feel that they aren't very creative. This is, of course, not true—everyone is creative in their own way. Help your child understand that creativity is about looking at things in new and different ways rather than about making a certain type of art or participating in a specific group.

DISCUSSION QUESTIONS

Who are the most creative people you know?

What makes them creative? How are you creative?

How can being a creative person be a benefit?

What can limit creativity? When do you not feel creative?

Do you have to be creative all the time, twenty-four hours a day?

How does being creative make you feel?

How can creativity help you in school?

❤ **NURTURE:** In order to foster creativity, it is important that we as parents give our children opportunities for undirected activities and play. It is often tempting to "help" our children play with their toys or games the "correct" way, and we can certainly help out when our children ask or to keep them safe. There is a certain value in letting them explore, get messy, and get excited by their own creativity.

Activity: Clear off the kitchen table. Set out a variety of art supplies that your child can use without assistance. Set out a stack of clean paper. Call in your child and set the kitchen timer for five to thirty minutes, depending on their age and ability. Tell them you are having a creativity party and that the only rules are to make as many items as they would like. At the end, select one to display somewhere in your home.

Activity: Gather several portable household objects (such as kitchen spoons, a duster, a measuring tape, a shirt, etc.) and place them in a pillowcase. Play "And Then …" with your child. Tell them you are going to take turns telling a story. Pull the first item out of the pillowcase and begin a story that uses the object in some way. After a minute, say "And then …" and pass the pillowcase to your child, have them draw out a new object, and continue the story themselves. Continue to pass the pillowcase back and forth until it is emptied and the story has reached its wacky conclusion!

⚜ **EMPOWER:** Challenge your child to a game of Pictionary or charades! As you play, compliment them on the creative ways they come up with to draw or act out their word.

CRITICAL THINKING

"RESPONSIBILITY TO YOURSELF MEANS REFUSING TO LET OTHERS DO YOUR THINKING, TALKING, AND NAMING FOR YOU; IT MEANS LEARNING TO RESPECT AND USE YOUR OWN BRAINS AND INSTINCTS; HENCE, GRAPPLING WITH HARD WORK."
– ADRIENNE RICH

📖 **EDUCATE:** Critical thinking always begins with a question. As we teach our children to ask questions and assess answers, we're teaching them to protect themselves against false information and predatory scam artists. But beyond this, we're also teaching them to engage more deeply with the information and conversations that are happening around them. Critical thinkers don't simply accept the world, they challenge it in productive, life-changing ways.

Q **COMMUNICATE:** Critical thinking skills are commonly emphasized throughout a child's formal education, and it is likely that if they are currently in school, they are somewhat familiar with the topic. However, it's important that our children recognize that we, as their parents, value this skill and want to help them practice and develop their critical thinking. In the long run, our children will be better able to live fulfilling lives if they are able to critically evaluate the information they encounter.

DISCUSSION QUESTIONS

Where can you go to get correct information?

How do you know if information is correct or true?

What does it mean for something to be true?

What does it mean for something to be biased?

What reasons might someone have for stretching the truth or even outright lying?

What are some questions you can ask yourself to use your critical thinking skills?

24

♥ **NURTURE:** There are many different models available to help us teach and reinforce the skills involved in critical thinking. One basic foundation lies in learning to ask questions.

For example, we can use who, what, where, when, why, and how questions to help ourselves think critically about a statement. Take a few minutes to discuss a news story, online article, political statement, or even a few quotes from a picture book. Ask your child what was said, who said it, how was it said, where it was said, when it was said, and why was it said.

Another way to help your child strengthen their critical thinking skills involves helping them make a prediction or a hypothesis, develop logical arguments, determine a conclusion, and evaluate or form an opinion.

Activity: Look through a magazine or at billboards on the road and ask your child what product the advertiser is selling. Ask who they are trying to sell it to and whether or not the child thinks that the advertiser is being completely truthful. Help your child see the ways that advertisers can distort reality in order to try to convince you that you need a product.

Activity: Have your child write a book review in which they assess and evaluate the story, using their critical thinking skills to determine whether or not the story was realistic. Have them present their review to you and see how well you are convinced!

◢ **EMPOWER:** Challenge your child to pick one of the following questions and answer it. There are no right answers; these prompts are designed to help them think outside the box, ask questions, and use their critical thinking skills!

CHALLENGE PROMPTS

Are you more like an ocean, a stream, or a lake? Why? What are the top three most important jobs and why are they important? How would you describe a tree to someone who had never seen one? If you could talk to a volcano, what do you think it would say? What would your life be like if you lived on Mars in a space colony?

INITIATIVE
"DO NOT WAIT FOR LEADERS; DO IT ALONE, PERSON TO PERSON." — MOTHER THERESA

📖 **EDUCATE**: **Initiative:** *the ability to assess and initiate things independently.* An essential part of taking initiative to accomplish something is recognizing an unmet need. Effective leaders notice that there is a problem and then take action to do something about it. In order to be in charge of our own life, we need to take the initiative to do things.

Our intelligence enables us to see a problem, think critically about it, and then take steps to solve the problem. But having initiative doesn't mean that we have to do everything all by ourselves. For example, if a pipe is broken, we notice that it's broken, conduct research (call a plumber, ask a friend how to fix it), and then either fix it ourselves or hire someone to fix it. It doesn't matter which approach we take—either way involves beginning with the initiative to fix the pipe and ends with the pipe being repaired.

💬 **COMMUNICATE**: Developing the confidence in ourselves to have initiative and to follow through helps us to strengthen our ability to live fulfilling lives. Help your child understand the value of learning to trust their own abilities and find safe and effective ways to follow their initiative.

DISCUSSION QUESTIONS

What do you think the word initiative mean?

Who are some people that you think demonstrate initiative?

How can initiative help you become stronger?

How do you take initiative in your life?

How do you feel when you take the initiative?

Is there anything in your life that you want to take the initiative to fix?

What's holding you back?

💜 **NURTURE:** Help your child understand that taking initiative in their own lives does not necessarily mean undertaking huge tasks. Instead, taking initiative might look like doing their homework without being asked, remembering to do their chores, offering to help a sibling, or even just raising their hand in class to answer a question.

Activity: Set a timer for five minutes. Tell your child that they get to make a choice to use those five minutes to start something that needs to be done. It's ok if they can't finish their task during the time. The point is for them to take the initiative and make a choice with what to do with their time. Afterwards, talk with them about how it went and how it felt to choose something and then do it!

Activity: Select a card game that your child likes to play and play a round or two. As you're playing, point out to your child the choices they are making and the consequences of those choices. Help them understand that they are in control of how they choose to play the game.

🔺 **EMPOWER:** Challenge your child to set an initiative goal for the week—have them pick something that they want to do by themselves and then encourage them to accomplish that goal (but don't do it for them)! For younger children, this could be something simple, like choosing their own shirt for the day. For older children, challenge them to think of something that seems a bit intimidating but that they'd really like to do, and then cheer them on!

ANYTHING IS POSSIBLE!

RESEARCH

**"RESEARCH IS TO SEE WHAT EVERY-BODY ELSE HAS SEEN, AND TO THINK WHAT NOBODY ELSE HAS THOUGHT."
- ALBERT SZENT-GYORGYI**

📖 **EDUCATE:** **Research:** *investigating a subject in order to discover information or new ideas.* We often think about the term research as referring to a long, intensive search or as something that we did when we were in school. But the reality is that navigating the complex variables and circumstances of our lives requires fairly constant research. Whether it's selecting a school, choosing an activity, or simply hiring a repairman, we research our options in order to evaluate which solution best fits our needs.

Our children will continue to live and grow in an environment that requires research skills. By teaching them not just what the answers are, but how to find them, we are helping them learn how to employ continual learning and application throughout their lives.

🗨 **COMMUNICATE:** Today, when we have a question, our first response is often to "Google it." The internet provides many resources, but we have to be careful: due to the open nature of the internet, the content available online may not always be the most reliable, or even safe. We need to teach our children to research using a variety of different methods and we need to teach them to ask proper evaluative questions regarding the material they find online.

DISCUSSION QUESTIONS

When you have a question, how do you find the answer?

Who are people you can ask for reliable information?

Where are places you can go to look for good information?

What do you do when you find two sources that give different information?

Can there be more than one answer to questions? How? Why?

Are you allowed to search for information online?

[If yes] What are websites that we can use in our family to do research?

[If yes] How do you know if the information you find online is true?

♥ **NURTURE:** Children gain confidence in their own abilities to problem-solve when they learn how to effectively research answers to their questions. By teaching and modeling intelligent research, we help our children become problem solvers and empower them to make their own choices.

Activity: Take a field trip to a local library. As appropriate for their age, show your child how they can find the information they are looking for. For example, show a young child where the picture books are and show an older child how the fiction books are alphabetized so that they can look up their favorite author. Show a preteen or teenager how the Dewey Decimal System works so that they can figure out where to browse for books on specific topics.

Activity: Places like YouTube can provide great resources, including many hobbyist tutorials. Pick a hobby or toy that your child is interested in (for example, drawing animals, building Legos, Transformers, paper airplanes, rubber-band guitars, juggling) and practice researching it on YouTube together. Point out the difference between advertisements and actual information. Help your child make independent judgments regarding the quality of the tutorials they see (they can even vote or leave a comment if this falls within your family's internet guidelines).

🦋 **EMPOWER:** The Internet isn't the only place to satisfy your curiosity. When you're seeking truth and to make happy choices, it's important that you get the information from the right place. When you receive misinformation, it can cause you to be more curious because it doesn't ring true. Create criteria you can use to know how to use your curiosity wisely gain information in healthy ways.

GROWTH

"BE NOT AFRAID OF GROWING SLOWLY,
BE AFRAID ONLY OF STANDING STILL."
– CHINESE PROVERB

📖 **EDUCATE:** The principle of growth is universal: in a certain sense, growth and change lie at the heart of what it means to be alive. Our lives consist of a constant process of renewal and change on a cellular level; it's no surprise, then, that our minds continue to grow and change throughout our lives as well. The problem with growth is that it can, at times, be quite frightening. We don't always know what to expect. We don't always understand what's happening to us.

We can teach our children to be empowered rather than apprehensive with regard to their own personal growth. We can teach them to be excited about all of the opportunities they will have in their lives and to celebrate the many ways that their individuality will challenge and shape them.

Additionally, we can teach them to harness the power of growth through the practice of application. When we learn to apply our knowledge, we can actively develop and shape our lives. We can help determine the direction that our growth will take!

💬 **COMMUNICATE:** During the following discussion, find out how your child feels about growth and talk about the challenges they face in their life. Help them see the ways the application of knowledge can help empower them to use their intellectual strength in positive ways.

DISCUSSION QUESTIONS

What does the word growth mean to you?

In what ways are you growing right now?

Is growth only physical, or can it also be mental or emotional?

How does growth make you strong?

What are you most excited about in your next year of life?

What happens when we know something but don't apply that knowledge?

How can applying your knowledge help you determine the areas and ways in which you will grow?

♥ **NURTURE:** There are many people who know that it's important to exercise, but they don't exercise. Knowing something isn't worth a whole lot unless we actually apply it in our lives. Help your child see how essential it is to apply correct principles.

Another way that we can strengthen our children and empower them to find new directions for growth is through teaching them the power of planning and goal-setting. Moving forward with a plan lends focus and direction to the process of growth and helps children see how they can take control and work towards goals in their lives.

Activity: Sit down with your child and have them draw a quick pattern out for you (for example, circle, square, triangle, circle, square, triangle). Ask them what comes next in the pattern. What would happen if they changed the next item? Would it still be a pattern? Help them understand that a pattern is similar to setting a goal and planning out the steps necessary to reach that goal. When we apply our knowledge in order to meet goals, we can create beautiful patterns and lives!

◣ **EMPOWER:** Challenge your child to select one goal they would like to achieve during the following week. Help them make a plan for their success. Talk about the ways they can apply knowledge they already have in order to reach their goal. For example, if the goal is to learn to shoot a free-throw, the child could make a plan to watch the neighbor who can already shoot free-throws, practice shooting them for ten minutes every day, and ask a parent or a sibling for help.

CURIOSITY

"CURIOSITY IS ONE OF THE MOST PERMANENT AND CERTAIN CHARACTERISTICS OF A VIGOROUS INTELLECT." – SAMUEL JOHNSON

📖 **EDUCATE:** **Curiosity:** *the desire to learn or know more about something or someone.* We live in an amazing world with millions of things to be curious about! Everyone experiences curiosity; curiosity can lead to critical thinking, to exploration, and to new discoveries.

A person who is curious will look at a situation and ask questions: Why is something a certain way? How did it get that way to begin with? What else does it resemble?

As we teach our children to ask questions and remain curious, we can teach them simultaneously to balance their curiosity with critical thinking. As parents, we want to help our children embrace their natural curiosity while ensuring that they are not put in harm's way.

Q **COMMUNICATE:** We all discover things. Some of them are helpful, good, and useful. Some of them make us sad or confused. It's important to remember that we are in control of our curiosity and not the other way around. In order to help your child understand the importance of curiosity, use the following questions to start a discussion.

DISCUSSION QUESTIONS
What does it mean to be curious?

What kinds of things are you curious about? What would you like to learn more about in your life?

Is it ok to be curious about things like drugs? (Parents, the answer is yes—that's how you learn about them!)

How can being curious help you learn?

When is curiosity healthy?

Can curiosity harm you? If so, how?

How can we use curiosity wisely?

❤ **NURTURE:** Trying out a new hobby is a great way to foster curiosity. But before jumping right in, we should be sure we are doing something safe by finding out more about it in order to make an informed decision regarding its benefits.

On the other hand, we have all heard of people who are curious about drugs and decide to explore the topic through actual drug use. However, jumping into something potentially dangerous and addictive can have severe consequences. This doesn't mean it can't be helpful to be curious about drugs. What's important here is understanding how to learn and have experiences safely.

Activity: Your child is naturally curious and they love to hear stories, so take advantage of these circumstances. Tell them about a time you were curious and the result that led to an awesome discovery! Don't be surprised if they ask for the story again—they'll enjoy the experience of sharing and connecting with you as well as the story itself.

Activity: Use the following chart to initiate conversations with your child regarding topics that naturally elicit curiosity. Help your child brainstorm healthy ways that they can nurture their curiosity and learn about these important topics. Remember, the topics are not inherently bad or dangerous, but they can lead to experiences with severe consequences if we aren't responsible in how we approach the information.

CURIOUS ABOUT	HEALTHY WAYS TO DISCOVER	UNHEALTHY WAYS TO DISCOVER
SEX	SAMPLE ANSWERS: TALK TO YOU PARENTS, OBSERVE PEOPLE WHO ARE IN COMMITTED RELATIONSHIPS	SAMPLE ANSWERS: WATCH PORNOGRAPHY, HAVE SEX
LIGHTNING	SEARCH ONLINE, ASK YOUR SCIENCE TEACHER	TRY TO GET STRUCK BY LIGHTNING
HOW SAND FEELS WHEN IT'S WET	STICK YOUR HANDS IN SOME SAND	PUT SAND IN A GLASS OF WATER AND DRINK IT
DRUGS	TALK TO YOU PARENTS, VISIT THE DARE WEBSITE, ATTEND A NARCOTICS ANONYMOUS MEETING	DO DRUGS

EMPOWER: Challenge your child to visit your local library in order to research a topic that they are curious about. Help them use the library's search engine and reference section. As an additional challenge, have your child talk to a librarian on their own, asking for further information on possible available resources. Teaching them to talk to and approach people like librarians and teachers empowers them to find out answers on their own!

RESOURCES

MEDIA

Calkins, L. (1998). Raising lifelong learners: A parent's guide. Da Capo Press.

Healy, J. (2011). Your child's growing mind: Brain development and learning from birth through adolescence. 3rd ed. Harmony.

Markham, L. (n.d.) How to raise an intelligent creative child. Aha! Parenting. Retrieved from http://www.ahaparenting.com/parenting-tools/intelligent-creative-child.

Pichea, A. (n.d.) 8 ways to foster a love of learning in your child. Retrieved from: http://www.raisinglifelonglearners.com/8-ways-to-foster-a-love-of-learning-in-your-children-2/.

Stipek, D. and Seal, K. (2001). Motivated minds: Raising children to love learning. Holt Paperbacks.

Trelease, J. (2013). The read-aloud handbook. 7th ed. Penguin Books.

Merriam-Webster's learner's dictionary. (n.d.). Retrieved from http://www.learnersdictionary.com/.

ORGANIZATIONS

Scholastic
{www.scholastic.com}
Scholastic provides educational materials especially for students.

Edutopia
{www.edutopia.org}
Edutopia seeks to change education for the better.

SPIRITUAL ACCOUNT

"WHEN WE SPEAK TO EACH PERSON GENTLY, WHEN WE DEAL WITH OTHERS HONESTLY, WHEN WE APPROACH THE WORLD WITH OPTIMISM, WE MODEL SPIRITUAL BEHAVIOR FOR OUR CHILDREN."
– YVETTE MILLER

INTRODUCTION

Why develop one's spirituality? Does spirituality mean that we have to believe in a god or religion? How does an understanding of the spiritual dimensions of human existence help strengthen a growing child?

There is a story of the Buddha in which he is asked by his followers about the source of suffering. In return, the Buddha relates the story of a man who has been shot by an arrow. It didn't matter to the man who made the arrow or what kind of wood it was—that type of knowledge wouldn't help stop his suffering. What mattered was knowing how to get the arrow out and stopping the pain. Developing a sense of spirituality does not mean subscribing to a particular religious view, but it can help you develop tools that can be used when you're "shot by an arrow." When there are challenges, pain, or difficult emotions, having a sense of your spirituality can help you have the strength to deal with these in a positive and healthy way.

The following six topics have been selected to help you introduce your child to a concept of their own spirituality and then help them find effective spiritual tools that will develop and strengthen their spirituality. It is likely that you as a parent have already introduced the concept of spirituality to your child. You may participate in an organized religion. You may consciously cultivate a secular humanism. You may not have thought much about spirituality explicitly. The content here is designed to work within your personal belief system, whatever that may be. We are providing a structure that will allow you to have helpful conversations with your child regarding the concept of spirituality generally, but the way you present the information in these conversations is entirely up to you as a parent.

Part of the reason it's important to have conversations regarding spirituality with your child is that:

1. It's like talking about sex—they're going to hear a lot of different information from a lot of different people and you want them to know that you are their primary source of information and that they can talk to you about any aspect of their spirituality.

2. Having conversations on personal, subjective topics gives your children an opportunity to connect with you on an important level; it also fosters open, thoughtful communication between parent and child.

3. People who have a high level of spiritual well-being, including children and teens, have been shown to be happier, healthier, and more emotionally stable than those without. The point isn't to force someone down a path of predetermined spirituality. The point is to open up a dialogue on an important topic in order to strengthen your child.

BELIEF

"A CYNICAL YOUNG PERSON IS ALMOST THE SADDEST SIGHT TO SEE, BECAUSE IT MEANS THAT HE OR SHE HAS GONE FROM KNOWING NOTHING TO BELIEVING NOTHING."
— MAYA ANGELOU

📖 **EDUCATE:** **Belief:** *a certainty that someone or something exists or that something is true.* Everyone believes things about the world they are in. Becoming aware of your beliefs gives you the ability to think about them, make decisions about them, and change them. When children realize that they can take an active part in their beliefs, they strengthen and plan their own moral and ethical approach to the world. Recognizing your beliefs empowers your own spiritual connection.

🗨 **COMMUNICATE:** What you think about something, even though you may not have personally experienced it yourself, can take the form of belief. For example, you can believe that the earth is round even though you haven't been into outer space to see for yourself. Help your children identify the beliefs that they currently have. This will help them see how their beliefs shape their understanding of the world.

DISCUSSION QUESTIONS

What does it mean to believe something?

What are some things that you believe?

How does _ (the answer from above question) affect your world?

Do you only believe in things you can see?

How could someone believe in something they can't see?

How can your beliefs make you stronger?

♥ **NURTURE:** Choose one or more of the big picture questions below and discuss with your child. Help them see that they already have beliefs. Make this an open discussion; there are no right or wrong answers.

BIG PICTURE QUESTIONS

What happens when we die?

Did we exist before we were born?

Why are we on the earth?

Why do people suffer?

Where does evil come from?

Activity: Discuss your family, friends, and acquaintances with your child. Write down the different belief systems you have identified and count how many you have listed. Teach them that people can believe different things and still live and work together. We respect other's beliefs and we respect and honor our own beliefs as a family and as individuals.

👑 **EMPOWER:** Challenge your child to learn with you about a belief system they don't currently hold (such as a religion). Compare what that belief system believes about a big picture topic (such as death) with your own family beliefs.

ATTENTION

"I HAVE LEARNED A GREAT DEAL
FROM LISTENING CAREFULLY."
– ERNEST HEMINGWAY

📖 **EDUCATE:** **Attention:** *the act or power of carefully thinking about, listening to, or watching something. It also refers to applying the mind to something.* We live in a busy, modern world. Learning to listen and pay attention to yourself is a skill; it is something you can practice and develop. Cultivating spirituality involves slowing down, sitting still, and taking the time to listen. Guided meditations, mindfulness, and awareness are ways that we can strengthen our abilities to concentrate, give attention, and listen.

💬 **COMMUNICATE:** Practice the following mindful meditation activity together with your child, then discuss the results using the following questions.

Step 1. Find a place where you can both sit down, such as on kitchen table chairs. Sit forward and straight on the chair so that your back isn't touching the back of the chair. Put your feet flat on the floor and rest your hands on your leg or loosely clasp them in front of you.

Step 2. Practice breathing in and out, paying attention to the breath as it goes in and out. How does it feel in your nose? In your lungs?

Step 3. Your mind will wander and chatter; you will quickly find that you are no longer thinking about your breath. This is normal. When this happens, practice returning your attention to your breathing. See if you can sit still, focused on your breathing for five minutes, ten minutes, or even fifteen minutes.

Note: It can sometimes help to count your breaths in and out up to ten (so that every odd number is a breath in and every even number is a breath out).

40

DISCUSSION QUESTIONS

What did it feel like to pay attention to such a simple thing as breathing?

Was this exercise harder or easier than you thought it would be?

What did your mind do while you were concentrating on your breath?

What do these reactions tell us about how our minds work?

♥ **NURTURE:** As with any skill, learning to concentrate through attentiveness takes practice. Attention is like a muscle—the more you use it, the stronger it becomes.

Activity: Take a walk together with your child—around the block, at a park; any location will work. As you walk, find a few minutes when you agree to walk silently, just listening to the sounds around you. Afterwards, talk about what you heard: traffic? phones? wind? birds? water? Ask your child what these sounds help them know about the place where you are walking (for example, sirens could indicate you're near a hospital, barking dogs could tell you you're passing by the neighbor's house, etc.).

Activity: Practice the mindfulness meditation activity outlined above with your child every day for one week, then check in with each other: is it easier or harder? How do you feel physically after those five minutes? Do you feel sleepy or happy? Do you feel calm or grumpy?

◣ **EMPOWER:** Challenge your child to practice paying attention through a simple mindfulness meditation on their own for one week. Discuss how these exercises provide a way to calm down both our mind and our emotions if we are worried or upset. Over time, with consistent practice, they will notice that their mind is more peaceful. If they don't enjoy practicing mindfulness, encourage them to try something like running, yoga, swimming, or another activity where they can practice paying attention to their body and clearing their mind.

CHANGE

"TO IMPROVE IS TO CHANGE; TO BE PERFECT IS TO CHANGE OFTEN." – WINSTON CHURCHILL

📖 **EDUCATE:** **Change:** *to transform or become something else, to replace a habit.* Change is a normal, constant part of living life. Things change, places change, people change. Cultivating spirituality can help us deal with changes in positive ways, even if we're not happy about the changes. Spirituality provides us with a sense of purpose or meaning.

Teaching a child to appreciate change in their life gives them a useful tool that strengthens their ability to live a healthy, balanced life. Many different spiritual practices provide a variety of means to assess change and try to make sense of it. We may not always understand why things change or even how those changes affect us, but we can learn to accept change in positive ways.

💬 **COMMUNICATE:** It's important to help your child understand that change is something constant in life. If they stopped changing, they would stop growing (and usually children like things that help them grow!).

Activity: Share with your child a time when you had to change for the better and ask them if there is a time they can remember going through a non-physical change, willingly or unwillingly.

DISCUSSION QUESTIONS

How have you changed since you were a baby?

Are these changes good, bad, or neither?

What would have happened if you had not changed or grown?

How do you feel when things change?

How do you react when you experience a good change? A bad change?

Why do you think things are always changing?

💜 **NURTURE:** Use the following activities to help your child recognize the positive aspects of change. Emphasize how they have grown stronger through the changes in their lives.

Activity: Look through pictures of your child from when they were a baby over time to their current age. Discuss the changes that have taken place. Ask them how they feel when something changes.

Activity: Plant a garden, even if it's just some seeds in a cup on the windowsill, and watch them change and grow. Measure their growth each day. Discuss the changes happening to the seed and whether they are positive or negative.

Activity: With your child, make some pancakes. As you are mixing the dry ingredients with the wet, point out the changes that are occurring in order to create the pancake batter. After you pour it onto the griddle, have your child watch with you to see what happens. When you flip over the pancake, it's clear that there have been some pretty big changes going on! As you enjoy your breakfast, talk about how change can be a positive (and delicious!) thing.

🪶 **EMPOWER:** Challenge your child to keep a regular journal. Help them set aside time to write either daily or weekly. Giving them a special book to write in or making journal time a family activity can bring a sense of importance to this activity. If your child doesn't know what to write about, prompt them to reflect on their recent experiences. What did they enjoy? What did they learn? What did they dislike? Even information such as what they wore or what they ate can help create a portrait of the person your child is becoming.

As part of this journaling challenge, encourage your child to periodically read what they have written (once a month, once a year). Over time, your child will be able to see how they have grown and changed.

COMMUNITY

📖 **EDUCATE:** **Community:** *a group of people who have the same interests, goals, residential area, religion, race, etc.* Spirituality connects us with other human beings, creating community. Spiritual people engage in practices that build connection and community, such as compassion, thoughtfulness, and forgiveness. Being able to connect with other people and participate in various communities not only strengthens our relationships, but shows us, to some degree, what it means to be a human being.

❓ **COMMUNICATE:** Help your child understand that we can belong to groups based on many things—education, sports, common beliefs, geography, or location. An essential element to a community is that there is a common theme that ties people together. Communities work together to accomplish goals that are larger than each individual.

There are many ways to join belief communities—religious congregations may be the most obvious, but joining volunteer groups, service organizations, clubs, etc., are other ways to consciously choose community. People in a community don't always agree but they often work toward a common purpose. We have to practice working together and getting along (also known as harmony).

DISCUSSION QUESTIONS

Who are people you feel connected to?

How do common interests help us form communities?

How can kids contribute to a community?

What should you do if you don't agree with someone in your community?

Can you be part of more than one community at a time?

💜 **NURTURE:** There is no one-size-fits-all approach to community connection; instead, as parents we want to help our children understand the ways that community strengthens them by providing opportunities for involvement rather than forcing participation. Give your child the opportunity to see themselves as part of something bigger than and outside of themselves.

Activity: Explore harmony with your child. Teach them a simple song round to sing, such as "Row, Row, Row Your Boat." Enjoy learning to sing the round together. Point out to your child how multiple voices participating at different times and in different ways creates something more complex and beautiful than singing alone. The name for this complexity is harmony. Discuss the way harmony works to create music and how people can work together in harmony to create community.

Activity: Have your child make a list of the various communities to which they belong, like their family, school class, sports team, or religious group. After they make their list, have them name several people in each group, like friends and coaches, whom they like and who make them feel good about themselves. Point out ways that participating in these communities strengthens them and gives them more people to connect with.

Activity: Take a walk in a wooded area or park with your child (this could be in the yard or in a forest). Have them gather up sticks and twigs as you walk. When you've gathered a fair amount, have your child select one twig and snap it in half, then bundle the remaining twigs together and have your child try to break them (it should be difficult, if not impossible). Teach your child that the bundle of sticks and twigs acts like a community: when we are connected with our communities, we are stronger together!

🐚 **EMPOWER:** Challenge your child to join a new community or strengthen an existing one. For example, if they enjoy reading, perhaps they'd like to participate in a local book club at the library or a bookstore. And of course, they are already part of a very important community—your family!

GRATITUDE
"IF THE ONLY PRAYER YOU SAID
WAS THANK YOU, THAT WOULD
BE ENOUGH."
- MEISTER ECKHART

📖 **EDUCATE: Gratitude:** *a feeling of appreciation or thankfulness.* Gratitude is a specific spiritual practice basic to every belief system. Expressing gratitude helps a person to think beyond themselves, find perspective, feel connection with others, and to feel joy.

As Melody Beattie says, "Gratitude unlocks the fullness of life. It turns what we have into enough, and more. It turns denial into acceptance, chaos to order, confusion to clarity. It can turn a meal into a feast, a house into a home, a stranger into a friend." When we teach our children to see their lives through gratitude, we are giving them tools to find peace, understanding, joy, and emotional connection.

💬 **COMMUNICATE:** Sometimes we make the assumption that everyone prefers to express and receive gratitude in the same way. And while it's true that saying thank you is a fairly universal way to express gratitude, there are other ways that people feel emotional connection. For example, some people enjoy giving a thoughtful gift or writing a card and mailing it to express their gratitude. Some people might take another person out for a meal, go to a movie, or go for a walk. Sometimes a simple hug or a peaceful prayer is the best expression of one's gratitude.

DISCUSSION QUESTIONS
How do you know when someone is grateful?

What are ways people say thank you?

Why is it important to say thank you?

What are you grateful for?

How do you feel when other people express their gratitude?

How do you feel when you express your gratitude?

♥ **NURTURE:** One way to deepen our gratitude involves putting ourselves in the place of another person. While we may enjoy giving gifts to express our gratitude, it is also a worthwhile exercise to think about who we are expressing gratitude to and what they might enjoy. The other person may really appreciate words and a letter saying thank you. The following activities are designed to help your child practice gratitude in ways that specifically strengthen their connections and bonds with other people.

Activity: Set a goal as a family to practice active gratitude each day. Active gratitude signifies consciously setting aside a few moments for reflection and expressions of gratitude during specific times throughout the day. For example, you may wish to practice active gratitude before a meal, before bed, after waking up, or at another time throughout the day. Talk to each other and encourage each other to remember!

Activity: Learn to write a thank you note. While writing a whole note to say thank you may seem challenging for a child, you can help them by teaching them this simple fill-in-the-blanks formula to write thoughtful, personal thank you notes.

MANY THANKS!!

DEAR _____ ,

SECTION 1
THANK YOU FOR _____
OR
I WANTED TO TELL YOU _____

SECTION 2 (*Compliment one to two things*)
I THINK YOU ARE _____ BECAUSE _____

SECTION 3
I HOPE YOU HAVE A _____ DAY.

SINCERELY,
_____

Activity: Play the Glad Game! When something difficult or challenging happens, we can play the Glad Game by looking for something to be grateful for in the situation. For example, if a storm has cancelled a soccer game, instead of being upset and pouting, help your child to think of a positive outcome (for example, maybe now we'll have time for that trip to the library).

EMPOWER: Challenge your child to select a person and say thank you to them for a specific thing. Bonus points for learning the ways they receive gratitude and using one of those ways!

LOVE
"LOVE IS LIGHT FOR THE SOUL."
– LAILAH GIFTY AKITA

📖 **EDUCATE:** The power and importance of love in our lives is self-evident. **Love:** *a feeling of strong or constant affection for a person, which can be romantic or platonic.* Love, in one way or another, often motivates our most important relationships. The love we have for our children pushes us into new situations for growth and learning, and more importantly, allows us to connect.

One of the ways that we can strengthen our spiritual lives lies in strengthening our actual ability to love. While love may seem at first glance to simply exist, the truth is that we can cultivate love through practice and care. Learning to respond with love during times of stress or confusion can bring great peace and often avoid behavior that might otherwise damage relationships.

The truth is that love is a powerful force. Love changes people. The sense of security, peace, and belonging that arises with both being loved and loving other people is an essential element of our human experience.

💬 **COMMUNICATE:** It is important for your child to recognize that there are many types of love: love for self, love for others; love as having care, compassion (a feeling of wanting to help someone), patience, forgiveness; love as empathy. Help your child understand that the underlying element that connects all the different facets of love lies in love's ability to turn our focus away from our natural self-interest and towards other people.

DISCUSSION QUESTIONS
What do you think love is?

Who are people that you love? Who are people that love you?

Who are people that you don't love? Why don't you love them?

How do you know who loves you?

Do you love everyone the same way?

How does being loved make you feel?

How do you love someone you don't know? Is that possible?

How do you love someone you don't like? Is that possible?

♥ **NURTURE:** Sometimes we find it really easy to love someone and to demonstrate that love. Other times, we may find it more difficult, especially when we fear rejection. Help your child learn how to develop and show love for others whose lives and circumstances are different from their own. Teach them that showing love is a strength that can change both their own lives and the lives of others for good.

Activity: Have your child reach out to someone and tell them that they love them. This can be done in person, but it also could take the form of writing a letter, a text, an email, Skyping, etc. The point here is to help your child realize that they are empowered to increase love and compassion in the world simply by not being afraid to appropriately demonstrate their care for another person.

Activity: We can actively nurture love through consciously practicing compassion. One way to practice compassion is to consider events from another point of view. You can practice compassion during your child's favorite TV show or movie! Help them practice putting themselves in one of the character's shoes, asking what they feel, and why and how their feelings might explain their actions. Explain that we can practice love by paying attention to other people and their needs, wants, and desires.

◢ **EMPOWER:** Challenge your child to read one of the following books and then follow through with the corresponding challenge in order to learn compassion and love for other beings.

Enemy Pie by Derek Munson (ages 3–8).
Challenge: Think of a way to make a friend out of an enemy (or just someone they don't like).

A Sick Day for Amos McGee by Philip C. Stead (ages 3–8).
Challenge: Do something to show love for someone who normally takes care of them.

Beryl: A Pig's Tale by Jane Simmons (ages 8–12).
Challenge: Do something to show love for a friend who is different in significant ways.

Wonder by R. J. Palacio (ages 8–12).
Challenge: Have a conversation with someone who is different in significant ways.

Confessions of a Former Bully by Trudy Ludwig (ages 8–12).
Challenge: Consider your friends. Can you think of one that you might have hurt in the past? Do you think you should apologize to them?

Out of My Mind by Sharon M. Draper (ages 10+).
Challenge: Get to know someone with physical or mental challenges and express love for them.

The Outsiders by S. E. Hinton (ages 12+).
Challenge: Make a friend with a person from a different group than they normally associate with.

RESOURCES

MEDIA

Cettina, T. Teaching spirituality to kids. Parenting. Retrieved from http://www.parenting.com/article/teach-spirituality-kids.

Fletcher, T. How to develop spirituality in your children. Retrieved from http://familyshare.com/how-to-develop-spirituality-in-your-children.

Hobby, K. (2008). Nurturing a gentle heart: Exploring spirituality with preschoolers. BookSurge Publishing.

Jenkins, P. (2008). Nurturing spirituality in children: Simple hands-on activities. New York: Atria Books.

Markham, L. 9 ways to foster kids' spirituality. Retrieved from http://www.ahaparenting.com/parenting-tools/character/spirituality.

Miller, Y. Six ways to teach kids about spirituality. Retrieved from http://www.chabad.org/theJewishWoman/article_cdo/aid/1915106/jewish/Six-Ways-to-Teach-Kids-About-Spirituality.htm.

Stonehouse, C. and May, S. (2010). Listening to children on the spiritual journey: Guidance for those who teach and nurture. Grand Rapids, MI: Baker Academic.

ORGANIZATIONS

Deer Park Monastery and Blue Cliff Monastery
{http://deerparkmonastery.org}
These monasteries have a wide range of programs that are designed for family participation, including young children.

Hartley Film Foundation
{http://hartleyfoundation.org/links}
The organizations represented here have various approaches to spirituality.

Spirituality & Practice
{http://www.spiritualityandpractice.com}
A multifaith and interspiritual organization that provides a large library of carefully curated resources designed to help others foster spirituality in their own lives and in the lives of others.

Spirituality For Kids
{www.spiritualityforkids.com}
This educational organization provides parents, teachers, counselors, and caregivers resources to help teach spiritual concepts to children.

Note: *Although spirituality and the religious are not the same, at times parents find it useful to participate in a religious community in order to receive additional support and guidance in cultivating spirituality in their home and in their child. Consider visiting different religious groups to find one that meets your needs as a family.*

EMOTIONAL ACCOUNT

INTRODUCTION

FREELY EXPRESS YOUR EMOTIONS IN APPROPRIATE WAYS SO THAT YOUR CHILD HAS A MODEL TO FOLLOW. SHARE METHODS YOU HAVE LEARNED TO SELF-REGULATE YOUR FEELINGS.

Most parents are well aware of the need to provide food, shelter, and clothing for their children and do an excellent job in those areas. However, we are often unaware of the critical need for us to create and nurture our children's emotional health.

- Teach specific habits and practices to help children to learn to identify and manage their emotions effectively. This will empower them to be resilient as they encounter the challenges and disappointments that all of us face.

- An important component of emotional health is how we interact both with ourselves and with others. We are better equipped to enjoy and manage relationships if we know our own emotional makeup and can be sensitive to the emotions of others.

- Teach the language of emotions. This is an important task for parents and caregivers. Children need to know how to identify their feelings and the feelings of others.

After these steps have been completed, ways to manage emotions appropriately should be taught.

Young children think in concrete terms and need to be tutored to recognize that an emotion that they would label anger has many underlying layers. We need to teach them to distinguish between frustration, annoyance, disappointment, embarrassment, etc., along with proper ways to express those feelings.

We need to model emotional health for our children. It has been said that the home we are raised in is the greatest classroom we ever attend. Parents need to be consistent in expressing their emotions in a positive way and helping their children do the same. Emotionally healthy people typically engage in daily practices that keep them balanced and develop positive outlets for their negative emotions, such as exercise, listening to music, playing with a pet, etc.

As children enter adolescence, they tend to separate from the family more frequently. As they become more independent, they form their own personal code of behavior. When parents teach and model emotional intelligence, their input maintains a significant weight as their children go through this critical process of identity formation. Our children may not always make the choices we would prefer; the best we can do is empower them with emotional intelligence, helping them understand and assume responsibility for their choices.

SELF-CONFIDENCE

**"ALL BEINGS HAVE INTERNAL, INFINITE, ETERNAL AND UNCONDITIONAL WORTH AS PERSONS."
- CLAUDIA HOWARD**

📖 **EDUCATE: Self-confidence:** *the ability to view myself as a person of worth because I exist.* Being confident in your abilities helps you share your gifts and talents to improve the world around you and stay on your chosen course. As you help your child to develop self-confidence, you help them develop emotional reservoirs they can draw on—you're helping them become stronger.

🔍 **COMMUNICATE:** It is important for you to understand how your child perceives other people's opinions of her. These perceptions and opinions affect her self-confidence and behaviors. This can also help you guide your child and build their self-confidence through family experiences and perceptions of the child. Use the following questions below to guide a discussion with your child.

DISCUSSION QUESTIONS

What makes you valuable?

What are your strengths?

What are your areas for growth?

Do you let other people influence the way you feel about yourself?

Why do you think it is difficult to separate your self-confidence from what others may think or say about you?

What advice would you give to a friend who is struggling with self-confidence issues?

How can you maintain your self-confidence in the face of people or situations that make you question your worth?

💜 **NURTURE:** As parents, we are naturally proud of our children when they succeed. However, we need to be mindful of the ways that we express that pride to our children. In order to help your daughter develop self-confidence, remember to include expressions of recognition that compliment her for her learning process as well as her achievements. The act of learning includes struggle, failure, trying again, and partial success. If we help our children understand that learning is a process, we'll help them gain confidence in the fact that they try things and work at them rather than focusing on achieving perfection.

SAMPLE DIALOGUE

Parent: "Wow, I'm really impressed with the improvement I'm seeing in your jump shot!"

Child: "Yeah, but I'm still missing most of them."

Parent: "You know, you're making more of them now than you were a week ago–and I know that as you keep practicing, you'll get even better. Your coach is going to be impressed with the ability you have to work on something so difficult!"

👑 **EMPOWER:** One way to help our children succeed in developing self-confidence is to set them up for success and then reinforce that success through recognition. It's ok to let a child show off now and then! Help your child gain self-confidence and understand how that self-confidence is developed with the following challenge.

Activity: Challenge your child to pick out a talent they have and display it or share it with others. It can be telling jokes, doing magic tricks, or doing a headstand. Keep it simple. Have them document how they felt as they shared this ability with others.

OPTIMISM
"THE GREATER PART OF OUR HAPPINESS OR MISERY DEPENDS UPON OUR DISPOSITIONS, AND NOT OUR CIRCUMSTANCES."
- MARTHA WASHINGTON

📖 **EDUCATE:** Positive thinking is a healthy practice that provides benefits for the body and the mind. **Optimism:** *A feeling or belief that good things will happen in the future.* Both our physical and emotional health are improved when we view the world and people in a positive light.

💬 **COMMUNICATE:** In order to help your child develop a more balanced understanding of the value of optimism, consider using the following questions to help guide a discussion.

DISCUSSION QUESTIONS
Why might it be difficult to stay optimistic?

Think about a time when you remained optimistic about a difficult situation. How did that affect your experience?

How can your optimistic attitude affect those around you?

What are habits of optimistic people?

How can I remain optimistic even when things don't turn out well?

♥ **NURTURE:** One of the ways that we can help our children cultivate an optimistic attitude is by providing them with a sense of confidence. If they believe that they are going to have a good experience, they will be more able to identify the positives of the experiences that they have.

Activity: Sit down with your child and list several things that she is apprehensive about. Discuss a positive phrase she can repeat when she feels overwhelmed (when taking a test or when a performance or game is coming up, for example). Practice saying a simple phrase like "I got this" or "I can do this." Be sure to sit down afterwards to discuss and document her experience with this exercise and work to be consistent with its application.

SAMPLE DIALOGUE

Child: "I'm so mad! Angie was going to come over to my house, but her mom said she had to go visit her grandma instead."

Parent: "I'm sure you're disappointed. But let's practice: what could be positive here?"

Child: "Nothing. This is dumb. I'm just mad!"

Parent: "Yes, but remember how Angie's grandma has been sick? What do you think about the fact that she's feeling well enough for visitors now?"

Child: "Yeah ... I know. It is good that Angie gets to see her. I know she's been missing her."

Parent: "How does thinking about how this is good for Angie make you feel?"

Child: "Well, I'm still really disappointed that we won't get to play. But I'm glad Angie's seeing her grandma. And now we have enough time to play Settlers of Catan tonight together!"

Parent: "Good job choosing to find a positive outcome here! I can't wait to play after dinner!"

EMPOWER: Newton's Third Law of Motion states that for every action there is always an equal reaction. For our children, this translates into something we are all familiar with: whatever the situation, our child will have an opinion and a reaction. Success in cultivating optimism lies in realizing that we have a choice when it comes to how we will react to a situation.

Activity: Challenge your child to learn to choose optimism by encouraging them to pause when they feel angry, upset, or frustrated by a situation. Select an activity they normally find frustrating (for example, doing a specific chore, practicing an instrument, or doing their homework). Give your child a bell or buzzer and let them ring it when they recognize that they are getting upset. Help them pause and find a positive outcome to the situation.

EMPATHY
"WHEN WE DO THE BEST WE CAN,
WE NEVER KNOW WHAT MIRACLE IS
WROUGHT IN OUR LIFE, OR IN THE
LIFE OF ANOTHER."
- HELEN KELLER

📖 **EDUCATE:** Sometimes people may isolate themselves, often limiting the number of personal interactions that they have. This is sometimes caused by spending too much time online or doing other solitary activities. While we all have different social needs, isolating ourselves can result in losing touch with one's humanity and the ability to relate well to others. We can sometimes forget that others feel real pain, and we don't react with love and empathy the way we should. **Empathy:** *the feeling that you understand and share another person's experiences and emotions; the ability to share someone else's feelings.*

Q **COMMUNICATE:** To help your child understand the concept of empathy, use the following questions to explore both their own emotions and their ability to understand the emotions of others.

DISCUSSION QUESTIONS

What does it mean to share someone's emotions?

Can you think of a time when someone helped you when you were experiencing a strong emotion?

How did that support help you at that time?

How did the support you received make you feel toward the other person?

How can you help others when they are having an emotional challenge?

How can helping people manage their emotions build a strong friendship network, family, and community?

❤ **NURTURE:** Take your child's natural temperament into consideration as you determine how to best help them learn empathy.

Activity: If you have an outgoing, extroverted child, he or she may always have a group of friends over but rarely spend time one on one with any one friend. In that situation, you could encourage them to invite a single friend over for a special activity, helping them prepare by encouraging them to pay special attention to their friend, asking them questions and carefully listening to their answers before responding. By helping your child learn to focus on and strengthen a specific friendship, you help them to increase their ability to add meaning and depth to their existing relationships.

Activity: If you have a child who is naturally more introverted, they may already be good at cultivating one or two strong friendships, but unintentionally cut themselves off from other potential friendships out a need to protect themselves from feeling socially overextended. Challenge your child to get to know one or two new friends in new ways. By helping them expand their circle of friends, you help them appreciate new perspectives and experiences and thus increase their capacity for connection and empathy.

Activity: Have your child choose a friend or family member that they would like to feel more empathy towards. Encourage regular interactions with this person. After each interaction, discuss your child's feelings for this person and help your child identify respective needs after spending time with this person. Help your child identify ways in which she could offer assistance or otherwise show them that she cares for them. Make this a regular endeavor.

EMPOWER: Challenge your child to think of someone they know who is sad, lonely, isolated, etc., and decide how they can show care for that person. Brainstorm ideas together, being sure to remind them to consider the person's situation and take that into account when planning a way to show their support for them. For example, your child could choose to write a letter, bake cookies, or simply smile at a clerk in the grocery store. Assist them with the follow-through and help them recognize how paying attention to their natural empathy strengthens their relationship with others.

POSITIVE SELF-TALK

"BE CAREFUL HOW YOU ARE TALKING TO YOURSELF BECAUSE YOU ARE LISTENING." – LISA M. HAYES

📖 **EDUCATE:** Everyone talks to themselves. Telling yourself "You can do this!" at the start of a difficult race or cheering yourself on at the end of a long day– "You got this"– is known as "self-talk." When we self-talk, we are literally talking to ourselves in our minds, hopefully in a manner that validates and encourages us. Sometimes self-talk can be harsh and downright harmful. We can teach our children that we are imperfect, but that we need to recognize that our mistakes do not define us. When we slip up, we need to gently remind ourselves that our behavior was out of character and we need to resolve not to repeat that behavior. Our self-talk should not be "You're an idiot!" but rather, "Next time I'll do that differently. Everyone makes mistakes."

💬 **COMMUNICATE:** Help your child learn to pay attention to their inner self-talk: in order to change anything for the better, we must recognize and evaluate what we are doing to begin with. These discussion questions are designed to facilitate this process to help your child establish healthy patterns of self-talk.

DISCUSSION QUESTIONS

What do you automatically say to yourself when you make a mistake?

Why is it important not be harsh with ourselves when we make a mistake?

Would you talk to other people like you talk to yourself?

What are some of the negative thoughts that you routinely have about yourself?

What do you think would happen if you started talking more kindly to yourself?

How could you work to replace your negative self-talk with positive self-talk?

♥ **NURTURE:** It can be difficult to change behavior patterns once we've already established them. If we know something is harmful—even if we realize on a logical level that negative self-talk is not good for us—it can be hard to actually stop that negative inner voice once it gets going.

Part of the way we can strengthen ourselves through positive self-talk is by A) learning to recognize triggers for negative self-talk, B) practice consciously changing our inner messages, and C) giving ourselves permission to praise.

Activity: Ask your child to write down a recent time when they used negative self-talk internally. What were the circumstances of that situation? Use the discussion questions above to facilitate this experience.

Activity: Gather your family or a group of your child's friends together. Give everyone a piece of paper and a pencil.
1. Have them write their name on the bottom of the page, then pass the paper to the person on their right.
2. When they receive a new paper, they should write something they admire or like about that person at the top of the page.
3. After the papers travel the entire circle, have each person open it up and read the list of compliments aloud.

Have them write their name on the top of the page. Pass the piece of paper around to each person. Everyone then takes turns writing something positive on everyone else's paper. Point out that everyone feels better about themselves when they hear good things about themselves, and challenge everyone to stop negative self-talk by replacing negativity by remembering this list!

👑 **EMPOWER:** Challenge your child to develop a word or phrase that they can use to help them when negative self-talk starts. They may choose a silly phrase that makes them laugh, a good memory, or simply a place they enjoy. Urge them to think of their word or phrase instead until that negative self-talk is quieted.

SENSE OF HUMOR
"BLESSED ARE THOSE WHO CAN LAUGH AT THEMSELVES FOR THEY SHALL NEVER CEASE TO BE AMUSED." - ANONYMOUS

📖 **EDUCATE:** **Sense of Humor:** *the ability to perceive humor or appreciate a joke.* Being able to laugh at ourselves and the situations that we get into is a great stress reliever and coping skill. We all face challenges and demands that are difficult and we all make mistakes. It is wise not to allow those problems to derail us, but to see humor in them. Model this behavior by practicing this habit yourself.

When we have a sense of humor, we can find humor in ourselves, others, and the situations we encounter in our lives. Developing that ability can help your child become more resilient, flexible, and better able to navigate difficult or potentially disappointing or embarrassing situations. We are stronger when we can find a way to laugh throughout challenges rather than giving up!

💬 **COMMUNICATE:** Children are often ready to laugh at anything and everything. Unfortunately, they sometimes learn the lesson that they shouldn't find humor in things because they've expressed their laughter in a socially inappropriate manner or context. Talk to your child about the positive aspects of humor and help them realize how having a sense of humor can make them strong!

DISCUSSION QUESTIONS

When things go wrong, are you more likely to get angry or laugh at the situation?

How does getting angry help you deal with the situation?

How does laughing help you deal with the situation?

Why do you think laughing at yourself and situations is beneficial?

What does it mean to laugh at yourself?

When is it appropriate to laugh at others?

When is it inappropriate to laugh at others?

Why do you think that finding humor in difficult situations can be difficult?

♥ **NURTURE:** How does one develop a sense of humor? Practice! Luckily the practicing can be pretty fun, especially if you're doing it with someone you love. Use these activities as an opportunity to strengthen your own connection with your child. Nothing builds relationships like laughing together!

Activity: Pull out your family's favorite funny movie and press play as you watch it together with your child. Sometimes kids need a little help to get some of the jokes (and sometimes they find things hilarious that we just don't get ourselves!), so take the time to help your child find the humor. After an especially good belly laugh, sneak in a teaching moment—point out how good, strong, and happy they feel!

Activity: Share personal stories of times you used humor to manage a disappointing experience. Ask your child to think of situations they have been in or could be involved in that would be easier to get through if they reacted to them with humor.

Activity: Put on some music and have a silly dance party—only funny, crazy, silly dance moves allowed! Laugh at yourselves together—it's a moment of family connection that creates both memories and resilience, along with making you feel relaxed, happy, and positive.

◣ **EMPOWER:** Challenge your child to practice using their sense of humor daily. Every day after school or before dinner, hold a "Chuckle Check-in." Tell each other about a moment during the day when you wanted to be mad, sad, or frustrated, but chose to use your sense of humor instead. Compliment your child on their growing ability to find strength in humor!

HONESTY

"TELL A LIE ONCE AND ALL YOUR TRUTHS BECOME QUESTIONABLE."
– ANONYMOUS

📖 **EDUCATE:** It is important for your child to understand how being honest helps them build stronger relationships. When we are honest, others learn that they can trust us. **Honesty:** *the quality of being fair and truthful.* Trust is a basic, vital component of any healthy relationship with oneself or others.

💬 **COMMUNICATE:** One thing that children may not understand is that true honesty requires being truthful with one's self as well as with others, regardless of the circumstances or environment. Help them understand that being honest with themselves builds emotional health and that honesty with others builds stronger relationships.

DISCUSSION QUESTIONS

What does it mean to be honest?

Can you think of some examples of honest people that you know?

What does it mean to be honest with yourself?

Why is honesty with yourself important?

Why is honesty with others important?

How can we be honest but also be kind?

Why would you want your family, friends, and teachers to think of you as an honest person?

What are the benefits of acknowledging our mistakes to ourselves and others?

♥ **NURTURE:** Cultivating honesty is a lifelong skill. Help your child learn to see the various ways honesty can strengthen their relationships through the following activities.

Activity: An often-overlooked aspect of honesty is honesty with one's own self. This includes understanding one's limits, making excuses for oneself, or knowing what will truly make us happy. Challenge your child to think of a time when they went along with something they knew wasn't right by making an excuse in their mind.

Activity: Select a book from our suggestions below and read it with your child. Discuss the story together, focusing on how the characters dealt with being honest. You can tailor this activity to your child's specific age and needs based on the book you choose!

Note: Please be sure to preview the book so that you can prepare for and anticipate the discussion you will have with your child.

PICTURE BOOK RECOMMENDATIONS (AGES 0-8)

The Boy Who Cried Wolf (multiple versions available). A well-known folktale of a young boy whose repeated lies about a wolf appearing land him in trouble when a wolf really does appear!

Ruthie and the (not so) Teeny Tiny Lie by Laura Rankin. A young fox finds something she loves, but her friend says it's his. At first she lies so she can keep it, but eventually tells the truth and feels much better!

The Empty Pot by Demi. A lovely tale of a Chinese boy who can't get the seeds given out by the emperor to grow. When he returns to the emperor empty-handed, his honesty is rewarded.

David Gets in Trouble by David Shannon. A young child finds out that not confessing to his actions can lead to consequences.

CHAPTER BOOK RECOMMENDATIONS (AGES 9–14)

Shiloh by Phyllis Reynolds Naylor. The story of an eleven-year-old boy who finds an abused puppy and has to decide if it's better to be truthful and return the dog or keep it and give it a happier life.

Harriet the Spy by Louise Fitzhugh. Harriet writes the unflinching truth in her notebook, but when her friends find it and read what she's written, Harriet suddenly finds herself isolated and lonely. How can she reestablish trust while being true to herself?

Nothing but the Truth by Avi. When a ninth-grade boy decides to hum along with the National Anthem instead of stay silent, his minor act becomes blown out of proportion. Great discussion of lies and truth.

BOOKS FOR TEENS RECOMMENDATIONS (12+)

While these books provide excellent and engaging material regarding ethics, integrity, and honesty, please pre-read to determine if the content is suitable for your individual child.

Code Name Verity by Elizabeth Wein. A captivating story of two young women during WWII.

Deathwatch by Robb White. When his boss accidentally shoots and kills an old prospector, Ben wants to report it but the boss does not.

EMPOWER: Challenge your child to a "completely honest twenty-four hours" contest. It can be trickier than we think! Join in the challenge with your child so that you can model how to catch yourself if you're not being honest. For example, an "Oops, that's not totally true, what I really meant to say was _____" can help your child learn how to recognize and correct instances of dishonesty.

RESOURCES

MEDIA

Cabrera, N., Shannon, J., and Tamis-LeMonda, C. (2010). Father's influence on their children's cognitive and emotional development: From toddlers to pre-K. Applied Developmental Science, 11(4), 208–13. Doi: 10.1080/10888690701762100.

Firestone, L. (2012, November 20). 7 tips to raising an emotionally healthy child. Retrieved from https://www.psychologytoday.com/blog/compassion-matters/201211/7-tips-raising-emotionally-healthy-child.

Goodsell, N. (2006). Factors influencing emotional health in children and teenagers. Retrieved from www.learninglinks.org.au/wp-content/uploads/2012/11/LLIS-01_Emotional-Health.pdf.

Knitzer, J., Lefkowitz, J. (2005). Resources to promote social and emotional health and school readiness in young children and families: A community guide. Columbia University Academic Commons. Retrieved from http://hdl.handle.net/100022/AC:P:9212.

Soclof, A. (2015, April 11). 4 ways to promote emotional health in kids. Retrieved from http://www.aish.com/f/p/4-Ways-to-Promote-Emotional-Health-in-Kids.html.

Tips to promote social-emotional health among young children. (n.d.) Retrieved from https://www.aap.org/en-us/advocacy-and-policy/aap-health-initiatives/mental-health/documents/se-tips.pdf.

Vann, M. (2009, December 22). Raising emotionally healthy children. Retrieved from www.everydayhealth.com/emotional-health/raising-emotionally-healthy-kids.aspx.

5 steps to nurture emotional intelligence in your child. (n.d.) Retrieved from http://www.ahaparenting.com/parenting-toolsl/emotional-intelligence/steps-to-encourage.

ORGANIZATIONS

American Academy of Pediatrics
{www.aap.org}
The American Academy of Pediatrics encourages optimal physical, mental, and social health and well-being for all children.

The Center for the Study of Social Policy
{www.cssp.org}
The Center is focused on working with families to build parental resilience, social connections, knowledge of parenting and child development, concrete support in times of need, and social and emotional competence of children.

Kids Mental Health
{www.kidsmentalhealth.org}
Kids Mental Health provides resources to help children be healthy.

Mental Health America
{www.mentalhealthamerica.net}
Their work is driven by their commitment to promote mental health as a critical part of overall wellness.

The National Parenting Education Network
{npen.org}
The National Parenting Education Network offers a parent education-based approach that allows for parents to gain additional skills and information to continually improve their parenting.

PHYSICAL ACCOUNT

INTRODUCTION
"IT IS HEALTH THAT IS REAL WEALTH AND NOT PIECES OF GOLD AND SILVER."
– MAHATMA GANDHI

The mind-body connection is something that is often overlooked in a person's overall well-being. People often see physical activity as a means to an end—a way to burn calories or maintain weight, or as a preventative measure to ward off aging and disease.

The benefits of being physically active and keeping your physical account full go far beyond just keeping the physical body healthy. Regular exercise and good nutritional habits have been shown to:

- Help manage stress
- Boost energy levels
- Counteract effects of anxiety and depression
- Promote optimism

Physical activity also provides an opportunity for family bonding while doing something good for ourselves. The overall physical health of a child includes much more than exercise. A strong child should feel good about the way his or her body functions. He or she will learn that eating nutritious foods not only keeps them healthy but helps them to feel like they're doing something great for their body. These things will help to grow and mold a child's healthy body image.

Physical activity itself can be a great coping skill for kids, giving them something to turn to in times of anger and stress and helping to calm them enough to deal with problems. As well, research suggests that physical activity among youth can strengthen resistance to addiction (see Volkow, 2011).

Physical wellness is an extremely important component to raising a strong child. The more active a child is, the better he or she will feel about their body as it grows and changes. Having and keeping their physical account full will help your child to be more equipped to deal with emotional and social issues as they encounter them.

BODY IMAGE

📖 **EDUCATE:** Body image is how we see ourselves when we picture ourselves in our minds, what we believe about our appearance, and how we feel about our bodies. Body image is an important part of our physical health because it plays a vital role in how we feel about our bodies as a whole. Having a healthy body image can help us feel confident in what our bodies are capable of.

💬 **COMMUNICATE:** Someone with a healthy body image appreciates the way their body looks as well as the way their body functions. People with a healthy body image are more likely to feel good about themselves as their bodies grow and change with puberty and other life events. They are also more likely to have a healthy sense of self-worth. These feelings and opinions can be influenced by other people and media sources.

DISCUSSION QUESTIONS

How do you feel about the way you look?

Where do our ideas about how we should look come from? From TV? From other people?

Why is being concerned about being a good person more important than worrying about the way we look?

Why is being healthy more important than fitting a certain mold of bodily perfection?

❤️ **NURTURE:** It's important to understand where our ideas about what is an "ideal" body image come from. It's also important to remember that what is "most healthy" can vary from person to person. Share experiences with your child about times when you feel your best. Are you eating healthy? Exercising? Are you comparing yourself to others? Why is it important to remember that comparisons can be dangerous? There are many different body types and shapes. We should know our worth and know that it is fixed, no matter what shape our bodies might take.

Activity: If your child is struggling with a negative body image, try this activity in addition to the affirmations: Challenge yourself and your child not to look in any mirrors (after preparing for the day) for one full day. Talk about how not looking at yourself during this time period made you feel. Insecure? Free? Less self-conscious? Discuss how not focusing on our appearance frees us to focus on other, more important values.

Activity: Have your child come up with five positive affirmations to say to him- or herself each day. The affirmations should be things your child specifically needs to remember throughout his or her day. Here are some examples:

I am kind.
I am a good friend.
I am an honest person.
I am fun to be with.
I will do what's best for my body.

EMPOWER: Everyone struggles with body image at some point in life. These struggles don't need to be permanent or change the way a person feels about him- or herself. If a person has a healthy sense of self-worth, he or she will know that even when struggling with negative body image, it shouldn't affect the way they feel about themselves as a whole person.

Activity: Ask your child to imagine that your body has changed in some way—a broken leg, for instance. Would this affect your self-worth? Should it? Does looking different change our worth as human beings?

PLAY
"IT IS A HAPPY TALENT TO KNOW HOW TO PLAY." — RALPH WALDO EMERSON

📖 **EDUCATE:** Play is engaging in meaningful, recreational activities that provide important developmental benefits for children. It has been said that play is the business of children. It is a critical way for parents to bond with their children and introduce the concept that fun is a necessary part of a balanced life. It is not reserved for children, but is a worthwhile practice to maintain across the life span. Play provides an outlet to escape our constant stressors and it contributes to emotional health.

💬 **COMMUNICATE:** In order to help your child develop a better understanding of the value of play, consider using the following questions to guide a discussion.

DISCUSSION QUESTIONS
What are your favorite play activities?

Is it good to play all the time or is work important too?

What is your favorite thing to play? Why do you like it so much?

What is one of your favorite memories of playing with your parents?

How can playing with your parents and friends improve your relationships with each other?

❤ **NURTURE:** One of the best ways to teach our children the value of play is to engage with them regularly in playful pursuits that are meaningful to them. These activities should be put on the calendar to be sure that consistency is maintained and so that everyone can look forward to spending quality time together.

Activity: With your child, brainstorm types of play that you can enjoy and schedule time for those interactions on a daily basis. It has been said that every day each parent should engage in play with each child in the family for at least fifteen minutes. The activity should be chosen by the child.

EMPOWER: It is also important for your child to learn to rely on their own imagination! Challenge your child to select an activity in which they can play by themselves for fifteen minutes. Set a timer to help them know how long they've been playing and congratulate them when they achieve their goal. Some activities for independent play include: write a story or comic book, build a model, play house, play school, create an artwork, shoot baskets, jump rope, play with building sets (such as Legos or K'nex), or set up a world!

HEALTHY EATING
"TO EAT IS A NECESSITY, BUT TO EAT INTELLIGENTLY IS AN ART." - LA ROCHEFOUCAULD

📖 **EDUCATE:** **Healthy Eating:** *choosing appropriate amounts of foods from the five food groups (fruits, vegetables, grains, protein, and dairy).* The timing of our eating, our food choices, and our portion size are all important components of healthy eating. Our eating habits are learned in childhood and are a major contributing factor to our physical and emotional health.

Q **COMMUNICATE:** In order to help your child develop a better understanding of the importance of healthy eating, consider using the following questions to guide a discussion.

DISCUSSION QUESTIONS

Why do we eat?

What are the advantages of eating healthy foods?

What kinds of foods and beverages are good for your body?

What kinds of foods and beverages are not good for your body?

Why do you think it's difficult sometimes to make healthy food choices?

How do you feel physically and emotionally when you are eating?

What do you think we can do to help both of us eat healthier?

♥ **NURTURE:** Maintaining a healthy diet is a learned behavior that parents model for their children. The eating habits that we establish as children have a powerful impact on our future relationship with food. Children need to be educated about how to eat wisely to maintain optimum physical health.

Activity: Healthy eating mini-activities for the whole family!

- Go into your pantry with your child and decide which foods are healthy and which are not.

- Read labels and discuss ingredients that are not good for our bodies.

- Discuss serving sizes.

- Ask your child to find nutritious substitutions for foods that are not desirable.

- Explore recipes for healthy meals.

- Let your child help you shop for groceries and prepare food that will be beneficial to him or her.

EMPOWER: Help your child realize that they have the power to make their own healthy food choices. Challenge your child to pack their own lunch for the next day! Depending on their age, they may need some guidance or assistance; for example, you can challenge your child to pack a lunch that contains all the colors of the rainbow or to pack a lunch that contains an item from each of the food groups. (Help them assemble the food and pack it as needed.) After they are done, check their lunch and compliment them on their healthy choices to reinforce their good decisions.

ADVENTURE
"LIFE IS EITHER A GREAT ADVENTURE OR NOTHING." – HELEN KELLER

📖 **EDUCATE:** The reason it's important for your child to experience adventure is twofold:

1. They'll be less afraid to try new things when they come along;

2. They'll be able to stretch beyond their comfort zone when called upon. Connections and bonds are formed when we try new things together—whether we succeed or fail isn't the point, it is the journey along the way. When we try new things we can achieve successes that we didn't know we were capable of before! There is strength in accomplishment and in trying new things both on our own and with our families.

💬 **COMMUNICATE:** Discovering new things through adventure creates wonder and helps our kids expand their horizons. It's important for your child to be able to stretch himself intellectually, spiritually, socially, or emotionally, but sometimes physical adventure takes more courage. Something that often keeps people from trying new adventures is fear.

Our children must learn to tackle their fears and anxieties. Because the biggest obstacle to trying is often fear, talk about ways your child can overcome this. Share a personal experience of a time when you overcame fear and doubt and did something amazing.

DISCUSSION QUESTIONS
What are some obstacles that keep us from trying new things?

What is a fear you have faced?

What is a worry or doubt you have that you'd like to overcome?

What is an activity you'd like to try but feel nervous about?

How can we see past our fears when we want to try something new?

How do we distinguish between real fears and the ones we create?

Are some fears caused by being afraid of what others think/say?

♥ **NURTURE:** Being outside and in nature is healing physically and spiritually and provides many opportunities for adventure. When our children have these opportunities, they learn to weigh risks and make choices. They won't always make the best choices, and this is why it's important to start off with small adventures and progress with your child's age and maturity level.

Activity: Pick a challenging adventure with your child—not dangerous, just challenging(perhaps walking to the park on her own or riding his bike to school, or something age-appropriate). As your child matures, move on to higher levels of adventure.

Level 1 Adventure Examples: Exploring a new place, hiking, biking, going on a picnic, bug identification, campout, going to a lake.

Level 2 Adventure Examples: Trying a new food, talking to new people, visiting a new state or another country.

Level 3 Adventure Examples: Set a long-term goal like running a long distance, swimming a new distance (with adult supervision), learning first aid, or learning a new skill like rock climbing.

Activity: Have your child choose an adventure and write his or her worries or fears about that adventure on a piece of paper, then throw it away or into a fire. Teach your child to let go of their worries or fears as the paper disappears. If possible, take your child to do the adventure they identified.

◣ **EMPOWER:** Challenge your child to set a goal and work on it for a month. Set small daily or weekly goals to help your child achieve this. For example, if my child was starting at a new school, I might encourage him to challenge himself to make a new friend each week. Daily and weekly goals might be to start with introducing himself or saying hello to someone new once a day.

EXERCISE

"PHYSICAL FITNESS IS NOT ONLY ONE OF THE MOST IMPORTANT KEYS TO A HEALTHY BODY, IT IS THE BASIS OF DYNAMIC AND CREATIVE INTELLECTUAL ACTIVITY." - JOHN F. KENNEDY

📖 **EDUCATE:** Whatever a child's fitness or comfort level, there is something he or she can do for his or her body that will benefit them physically, emotionally, socially, intellectually, and even spiritually.

The term "mind-body connection" indicates how thoughts, feelings, beliefs, and attitudes can positively or negatively affect biological functioning. In other words, our minds can affect how healthy our bodies are! In return, the physical health of your child can also affect their moods, behaviors, and psychological well-being.

Let your child explore the sports he or she enjoys most. Your child does not necessarily need to stick to a sport. As you discuss their options for physical activity, check yourself: are you trying to live vicariously through your child? Do you want your child to learn how to finish something, or is it more important to build a lifetime habit of exercise and great health?

💬 **COMMUNICATE:** Teach your child that the many benefits of exercise include increased circulation, regulation of sleep cycles, increased energy, and increased euphoria (you just feel better!) from the heightened release of endorphins.

DISCUSSION QUESTIONS

What activities do you enjoy doing in PE class? What don't you like?

Are there parts of your body you would like to be stronger? What are ways you think we could work on that?

Can we set a goal to spend thirty minutes outside each day together?

If you could pick any game to play outside, what would you pick?

♥ **NURTURE:** As you work together with your child to encourage healthy physical habits and increase their trust and confidence in their physical abilities, you will build strong bodies and strong relationships. Don't worry about your own physical limitations—the most important thing is that your child sees you challenging yourself. When we prioritize physical well-being in a healthy, balanced way, we demonstrate the importance of self-care for living strong lives.

Activity: Change an ordinary card game into an opportunity to grow stronger! Play Uno Workout: a yellow card = perform push-ups; a blue card = run in place; a green card = jumping jacks; and a red card = crunches. Fill in your own actions for wild cards, reverse, draw two, and skip!

Activity: Help your child figure out what they enjoy and what their strengths are by setting up an obstacle course complete with standing jumps, various ball throwing, running, crawling, and balance challenges. Take this activity a step further and complete the course yourself—participating in physical activities with your children strengthens both bodies and emotional bonds!

◤ **EMPOWER:** Help your child build a habit of wellness and fitness for life! Try new activities—of course, you can encourage your child to learn to play a sport, but be sure to play with them too so that you can have fun together.

Activity: Challenge your child to choose toys and games that encourage physical activity for an entire day. For example: balls, kites, jump ropes, roller blades, tag, hide and seek, sprinklers, frisbees, bats and baseballs, bikes, and scooters. All of these can keep them moving and entertained. When they succeed, consider rewarding them with special one-on-one time or a new physically-oriented toy to encourage more physical play.

As you work on developing healthy physical habits, don't give up if your child gets discouraged! The point here is to find out what will motivate your child. There are literally thousands of ideas out there with different activities and games—the point is to just do something! Find out what works for your family and get moving!

ADDICTION
"THE OPPOSITE OF ADDICTION IS NOT SOBRIETY. THE OPPOSITE OF ADDICTION IS CONNECTION."
- JOHANN HARI

📖 **EDUCATE:** Addiction does not just refer to substances. New neurological research shows how food, gambling, video gaming, and pornography can affect the brain—literally changing the way it works.

Addiction is a condition that results when a person ingests a substance (for example, alcohol, cocaine, nicotine) or engages in an activity (for example, gambling, gaming, pornography use, shopping) that can be pleasurable but the continued use/act of which becomes compulsive and interferes with ordinary life responsibilities such as work, relationships, or health.

When we help our children establish early patterns of healthy neuro-pathways, coping skills and healthy habits, we increase their ability to find satisfaction in non-addictive behaviors.

💬 **COMMUNICATE:** It's important for your child to understand that everyone's body craves constant dopamine release and pleasure, especially in times of distress. Understanding coping mechanisms and what triggers them can help a child take charge of their own behavioral choices. Our children need to recognize when coping occurs and what triggers their need to cope. We can help them come up with positive coping methods to deal with reactions such as boredom, stress, sadness, fear, loneliness, and anger.

> **COPING IS AN ACTIVITY WE DO TO SEEK AND APPLY SOLUTIONS TO STRESSFUL SITUATIONS OR PROBLEMS THAT EMERGE BECAUSE OF OUR STRESSORS.**

DISCUSSION QUESTIONS
What do you do when you feel bored or tired?

What are the things that make you stressed or worried? How do you handle these emotions?

Do you remember the last time you were angry? What did you feel like? What did you do?

Have you ever been really sad? What makes you sad? What makes you feel better?

What are other ways you could deal with things like being tired, sad, or stressed?

Have you ever heard the term coping mechanism? What do you think it means?

Can you think of negative ways some people choose to handle their difficult emotions?

What are some reasons people may choose to do things they know are harmful to their bodies?

How could knowing about your coping mechanisms help you deal with difficult emotions or situations?

IDEAS FOR CHANGE
You can help to change your child's habits and make healthy choices by changing their environment. When there are sweets and cookies available, that is generally what a child will choose. But if fruit is available, they will choose that. Kids get bored—if they have a trampoline, they will use it. If they have a television, they will use it. We can make it easier for them to make healthier decisions by providing better choices.

Activity: Set a goal to replace something that isn't working so well in your life with a better choice. Write it down and set small daily and weekly goals to change your habit. Give yourself time to accomplish the goal and recognize your small achievements along the way.

❤ **NURTURE:** Addictive tendencies exist in everyone. People can even become addicted to what are generally positive behaviors, like exercise, work, sex, shopping, and bargain hunting. The key is understanding when to say when.

One of the best ways to help your child avoid addiction is to keep them engaged and active. Kids have a lot of inherent energy. Help them to channel it toward positive activity. It's important for your child to understand what is dangerous about addiction! It may not be the substance or action (shopping, video gaming), it is the resulting state of disconnection from those around them and the compulsive behavior it causes.

Activity: When your child returns from a stressful situation like school, try employing a de-stressing technique before your child heads for the fridge, TV, or digital device. Offer to play a board game or go for a walk. Use healthy, enjoyable ways to de-stress and your child will be less likely to turn to mindless, unhealthy, addictive activities to wind down and relax.

Activity: After a healthy, fulfilling meal, talk about how delicious it was. Ask your child if they might enjoy seconds or thirds. Talk about how people often think that more of something that gives them happy feelings will produce more happiness and how this is not so. Use this example to describe the cycle of addiction to your child.

Activity: Play Hot Potato by placing all the phones and devices in one place. The first person to pick up a device has to suggest a game the whole family can play together.

🔱 **EMPOWER:** Most of us have one or more negative habits that need replacing, so join your child in a challenge to change! The point is to connect with your child as you challenge yourselves to change together. Remember, when he or she feels connected, they are empowered to avoid turning to unhealthy sources to feel that connection.

RESOURCES

MEDIA

Nutrition & fitness center. The Nemours Foundation. Retrieved from http://kidshealth.org/parent/centers/fitness_nutrition_center.html.

Fitness. American Academy of Pediatrics. Retrieved from https://www.healthychildren.org/English/healthy-living/fitness/Pages/default.aspx.

Volkow, M.D., N. (2011, March 1). Physical activity may prevent substance abuse. Retrieved from http://www.drugabuse.gov/news-events/nida-notes/2011/03/physical-activity-may-prevent-substance-abuse.

Denshire, J. (2011). Exercise (Healthy Habits). Mankato, MN: Smart Apple Media.

Bellisario, G., & Kurilla, R. (2014). Move your body: My exercise tips. Brookfield, Connecticut: Millbrook Press.

Rockwell, L. (2009). Good enough to eat: A kid's guide to food and nutrition. New York, New York: HarperCollins.

ORGANIZATIONS

KidsHealth
{http://kidshealth.org/}
KidsHealth is a great resource for parents and kids to learn about bodies, health, and behavior.

Let's Move!
{www.letsmove.gov}
Let's Move! is an initiative dedicated to fighting childhood obesity.

MEND Foundation
{www.mendfoundation.org}
MEND stands for Mind, Exercise, Nutrition, Do It! MEND encourages making healthy nutritional and lifestyle choices.

Mayo Clinic
{www.mayoclinic.org}
Mayo Clinic's Healthy Lifestyle page provides information and
tools for a healthy lifestyle.

If you enjoyed this book, please leave a positive review
on amazon.com

For great resources and information, follow us:

www.educateempowerkids.org
Facebook: www.facebook.com/educateempowerkids/
Twitter: @EduEmpowerKids
Pinterest: pinterest.com/educateempower/
Instagram: Eduempowerkids

18497535R00056

Printed in Great Britain
by Amazon